Anna's Book

Available as a Fount Paperback

MISTER GOD, THIS IS ANNA

Anna's Book

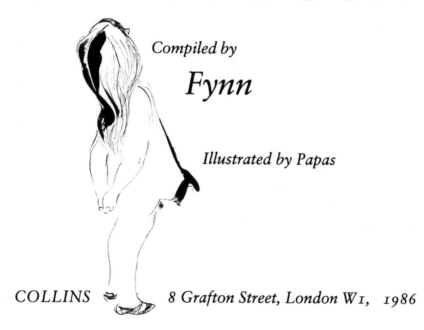

Compiled by

Fynn

Illustrated by Papas

COLLINS   8 Grafton Street, London W1,   1986

William Collins Sons & Co. Ltd
London · Glasgow · Sydney · Auckland
Toronto · Johannesburg

First published 1986
Copyright © Fynn 1986
Illustrations © Papas 1986

ISBN 0-00-217703-X

Set in Linotron Sabon by
Rowland Phototypesetting Ltd
Bury St Edmunds, Suffolk
Made and Printed in Great Britain by
Robert Hartnoll (1985) Ltd., Bodmin, Cornwall

CONTENTS

FOREWORD

In *Mister God, This is Anna* Fynn told the story of his friendship with this extraordinary child, and of her relationship with "Mister God" and the world around her.

Anna's story, with its timeless truths, lives on in the minds and hearts of countless readers. But after her death, little was left of Anna herself – except the abiding memory of her presence, and a few treasured fragments of her writing. In *Anna's Book* Fynn shares these with us.

Anna's spelling and punctuation were, like herself, uniquely original and exuberant. In a few places we have altered these slightly, for the sake of clarity, but in no way do these alterations detract from the flavour of Anna's language.

The Publishers

INTRODUCTION

I told the story of Anna in "Mister God, This is Anna". This is how it was. Anna and I found each other in one of those pea soup, foggy nights in November. I can't remember the precise date, it was probably in 1935. I used to wander around the docklands of East London night after night. It was a nice quiet thinking place, and often I needed to think.

It wasn't at all unusual to find a child roaming the streets at that hour – in the 1930s it was just like that. When I had taken her home, and after she had washed the dirt from her face and hands, I really saw her – a very pretty little red-haired child, but as she later told me "that's on the outside". It took me a very long time to know her on the inside, as she demanded to be known.

The relentless pursuit of beauty engaged the few short years of Anna's life. It was at first a little strange to be told that a picture smelt good, but I soon got used to that. Anything that delighted all your senses at once was, for Anna, God! And the microscope was a special way of seeing him.

So it was that Anna found God in the strangest of places – tram tickets, grass, mathematics and even the dirt on her hands, and then somebody told you to wash it off!

Whatever satisfied Anna's idea of beauty had to be preserved, written down by anyone who was prepared to do so, and saved in one of her numerous shoe boxes. Every so often these boxes were placed on the kitchen table and the contents sorted out.

Where she got the idea of beauty I do not know. In those years the East End of London was, for most people, a grimy, dirty place, but for Anna it was just beautiful. Anna spent most of her efforts in turning the ugly into the beautiful. This often meant inventing a whole new situation into which the ugly facts could be transformed.

It was beauty that really drew Anna and me together. I can't remember a time in my life when I haven't been totally absorbed with the subject of mathematics. In fact, I'd rather "do" mathematics than eat or sleep. Old John D., who taught me mathematics for seven years, once defined it as "the pursuit of pure beauty". Although I liked that as a definition, it wasn't until Anna had been with us for about two years that I really grasped what that meant. Anna and I were sitting at the kitchen table whilst I was working out the reciprocal of seventeen, which is another way of saying one divided by seventeen, which in the nature of things gave me another number, which was what I was after. A little while later it occurred to Anna to ask what happens if you divide one by the number you've just found? We worked it out the hard way. The answer was seventeen!! So often we sat at the kitchen table, Anna sitting on her curled up legs, chin cupped in her hands, whilst we "worked out things".

One evening, after we had been doing things on pieces of paper, she suddenly announced "It is just beautiful ideas". I don't accept that entirely, but I do accept G. G. Hardy when he says "there is no permanent place in the world for ugly mathematics".

Although I was considerably older than Anna, this pursuit of pure beauty made us companions in our explorations.

Her life was a continuous quest for knowledge and understanding as well as for beauty. Any thing or person that could answer her questions would be stored in boxes or asked to "write it down big". This request to "write it down big" did mean that her collection of writings were often spelt in various ways – not always right – but that didn't really matter. Often what had been written on her bits of paper were the kinds of things that grown ups would say. Adults's words on the lips of a six year old child were a bit puzzling at times, but Anna worked on the basis of "if it says the right thing in the right way, use it, if not scrap it".

During the years that Anna lived with me and my Mum and our changing household she wrestled with words and sentences to fit her ideas. It took me some time to realize that although we lived in the same world we saw it in different ways. Everything was for Anna a means of understanding "what it was all about". Grown ups had called her jackdaw, or parrot, little monkey, sprite – she was certainly all of these things but, more than these, she was a child.

1

Not Going To Church and What Mister God Is Like

Although Anna went to Church and Sunday School she was often more than a little irritated by this experience. It didn't seem to matter to her that God was meant to be the Creator, all powerful and loving, etc. Anna saw God as something other than this. God wasn't good because he loved or was just. God was good because he was beautiful. The very nature of God was pure beauty.

It was at first a bit of an ordeal taking Anna to Church, for it was the chess board flooring that grasped her, more than any preacher's words. As she once told me "it makes you tingle all over", and whatever made you tingle all over was very close to God.

What bothered Anna so much about going to Church was the fact that so many people seemed to be looking for miracles. For Anna everything was a miracle and the greatest miracle was that she was living in it.

I dont like to go to cherch very much and I do not go becase I do not think Mister God is in cherch and if I was Mister God I would not go.

Peple in cherch are miserable becase peple sin misrable songs and misrable prers and peple make Mister God a very big bully and he is not becase he is not a big bully becase he is funy and luving and kind and strong. When you look to Fin it is like wen you lok to Mister God but Fin is like a very baby God and Mister God is hunderd time bigger, so you can tell how nice Mister God is.

Anna divided numbers up into People Numbers and God Numbers. People Numbers were fairly easy to understand and fairly easy to work out. On the other hand, God Numbers were even easier to understand, but sometimes impossible to work out.

Anna seldom played with what would be recognized as the usual toys these days. The exceptions to this were her rag doll, her paints and my old train set. This consisted of one engine, one coal-tender and eight trucks. She played with them for about a week and then put them back into the box.

It was at this point that God Numbers started to appear. Anna asked, "How many different ways can I join together the engine, the coal-tender and the eight trucks?" I told her how to arrive at the answer. It turned out to be somewhat bigger than she anticipated and so she thought the final answer went into the realm of God Numbers. It was 3,628,800 and this was merely the result of finding out how many different ways ten articles could be arranged in a straight line. It didn't take her very long to realize that there would be a lot of questions with People Numbers that were going to land you up to your neck in God Numbers.

Peple says Mister God is like a king but fancy King Gorge coming down our street, I bet he do not know were our stret is is and I bet he do not know me. But Mister God know, Mister God know our stret and Fin and Mily and Twink and Pilet and all the darling flotkins. And I bet Mister God know the mark on my face even.

Anna had many friends in the neighbouring streets. Two of them were a little girl about four years old, Pilet, who was often called "Pill" and her baby brother William, who was always known as "Twink". All the children were known as "flotkins". The poor of the East End were often referred to as "the flotsam of society". Anna's friends Henriques and Niels called the kids "die Kinder" and the two words became "flotkins".

Because of the poverty in the East End at that time it was rare that any child had a new toy; most of the time it was a question of pretending that cardboard boxes could be anything you wished them to be. Many of the younger children joined in these games of "let's pretend".

One of the things that I had made was a device for blowing bubbles. With this I could produce a constant stream of fairly large soap bubbles – these the children would chase and burst with their hands, cricket bats, rolled up newspapers, etc. Twink's special instrument was a wire fly swat. Although these games could and did last as long as an hour or two, some of the children saw in these bubbles all the colours of the rainbow and realized the beauty of them. Some, Anna in particular, saw reflections. It was my efforts to explain to Anna just how these reflections came about that made me buy a garden globe for her. This garden globe was about eighteen inches in diameter, made of silvered glass. She soon realized that the images at the edges of the globe were, to use her own words, "squashed up". What was never and could never be seen as a reflection in this global mirror was the bit behind the globe. It was for Anna an indication that it was here that Mister God lived.

Anna put together the ideas of the garden globe, soap bubbles, glass Christmas tree decorations and finally highly polished ball bearings, which did exactly the same kind of thing, as everything could be reflected in a small ball bearing – that is, except the bit where Mister God lived. It was clear to Anna that everything that God had made could be reflected in a ball bearing. Being such a tiny thing it could easily be put in your pocket or even your ear, couldn't it?

I did not go to cherch on Sunday becase I did not want to go and Fin tuk me on a trane to a big forist. It is a wondfull forist and Fin cudle me and tell sum wondfull story about Mister God and it was better than Sunday school. In cherch people make Mister God big and big and big and Mister God get so big that you dont know, but Fin make Mister God so little, he get in your eye.

This would have been Epping Forest.

In the forist I see sum rabit and sum bager and a lot of bird and sum deer and a ded one too, but I did not see no peple becase they was in the boozer and wen I saw the ded deer it make me cry a bit and Fin say it is sily to cry for ded

thing but I can cry for peple in the boozer. Fin say to tuch the ded deer and I tuch the ded deer and it Puft like face powdr all up my nos. Wen it gos all to powdr it gos into dirt and then the gras gros in it and then the shep eat the gras and then I eat the shep and so I eat the ded deer and because Mister God make it all, I eat Mister God all time like the people do in cherch. But mine is better becase I do it all the time. Not only sometimes like they do in cherch but every time.

One of Anna's problems was the fact that things had a habit of changing shapes, from frog spawn to frogs, from caterpillars to butterflies; dead rabbits she had seen in Epping Forest certainly changed their shapes. Even the house near to us with the green painted woodwork, the house that Anna called the "green house" was slowly changing its appearance and shape. It seemed to Anna that everything needed its shape to live in. I could, of course, have tried to explain the word "decay" but I didn't. Anna concluded that when a thing changed its shape it was because it had something else to do for Mister God. For Anna, death was just one of those things that happened. Death was that point in life when you began to change shape. Anna and I had sat by old Granny Harding as she died; changing shape sometimes took a long time, a very long time. Even if Anna never knew what shape Granny Harding changed into, who would argue with her? Not me. After all, if Mister God wanted it, it must be good.

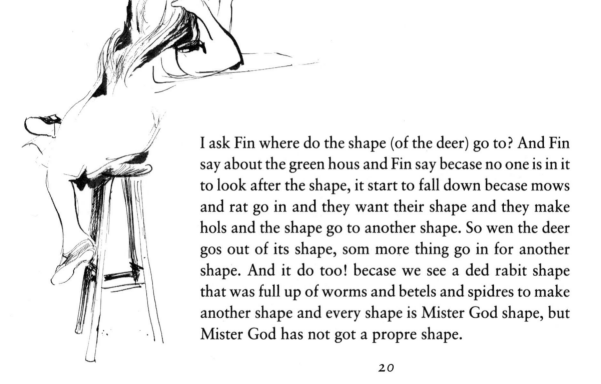

I ask Fin where do the shape (of the deer) go to? And Fin say about the green hous and Fin say becase no one is in it to look after the shape, it start to fall down becase mows and rat go in and they want their shape and they make hols and the shape go to another shape. So wen the deer gos out of its shape, som more thing go in for another shape. And it do too! becase we see a ded rabit shape that was full up of worms and betels and spidres to make another shape and every shape is Mister God shape, but Mister God has not got a propre shape.

Mister God is like a pensil, but not like a pensil you can see, but like a pensil you can not see, so you not see what shape it is, but it can draw all the shapes ther is and this is like Mister God. When you grow up you get a bit funy because you want Mister God to have a propre shape like an old man and wiskers and wrinkels on his face but Mister God do not look like that.

When Twink play tranes, he have a big wood box. Sumtime the box is like a trane and somtime lik a house and sumtime like a ship and sumtime like a car and sumtime you put sum thing in it and sumtime you do not, but you take sumthing out. And the box is like Mister God. Sumtime it luk like sumthing and sumtime it luk like another thing. If you say Mister God is green then Mister God cannot be red, but he is. If you say Mister God is big, how can you say Mister God is litle, but he is. And if you say Mister God is fat, you can not say Mister God is thin, ha! ha! ha! but he is too so!

21

How can you say of Mister God, becase you can not. But I can becase I have a sekrit book Fin give to me. It is a pictur book all about snow flak and every snowflak is not the same. If you look at a snowflak shape it is not the same as another snowflak shape, so it has not got a propre snowflak shape. But you can only call it snow and you can not call it a shape and you see THAT IS LIKE MISTER GOD. You can not call Mister God a thing and you can not call Mister God a shape and you can only call Mister God Mister God.

2

My Darling Mummy

As Anna began to grapple with her ideas and those very important things she had asked people to write down for her, she began to weave them into little stories. Everything had to be looked at and questions had to be asked. Her questions flowed like a flood tide around and over everything. All this activity made me glow with some pride.

While she sorted through her store of ideas and pieces of paper contained in her numerous shoe boxes, I had to admit to myself that there was indeed something a little strange about Anna. She had no strange powers, no special senses, no special abilities or anything like that. Now, about half a century after her death, I can see that she had the strangest of all qualities. She could WAIT. Wait for the right moment, wait until, for her, everything was just right.

I'm fairly certain that Anna had never been seriously abused. Badly neglected, yes. Badly treated, yes. But, Anna still kept hold of her idea of the perfect mother.

Anna's "Darling Mummy" was no real person, but something like putting together the jig-saw of the many stories she wrote about her ideas. Her waiting was like cooking – the mixture of the various bits came out as a different dish.

Before I go to sleep I think about Mummy and this is what I think. Did you ever see stars on a frost nigt? They look very clos and it is like they are tide to you with string and yor feet dont tuch the ground and you have not got any wate and when I luk in Mummy eye it is like I have not got no wate and if Mummy dont hold me tite I shall go up in the air like a bird.

Did you ever bump into a spidre web when you didnt no and did you ever go asleep on the cul gras and did you ever have a hot drink when you was cold and tired and did you ever strok a duk's tummy? Well, when Mummy kiss you, it is like that. Sumtime Mummy lips is delekat like a spidre web. Sumtime cul lik gras and sweet. Somtime hot and berning like soop and somtime soft lik a duk tummy very smooth. And when you kiss you have to put yor lips toogethre and so Mummy breeths on you and it smel like all the flowrs in the world and you can tell becase that is wot luv smell like so you can tell how luvly Mummy is.

If you see a funy thing you larf out lowd, but if you have a spesial sekrit insid you, you dont. But you have a spesial smile. And this is like a flower bud that is just going to open, you cant see it but you no it is so butefull inside. And Mummy smile is like that, but you cant see all the flowrs in the world at the sam time. So then Mummy dont smile all her secret smile at the sam time and I am very pashent because Mummy has got milions and milions of sekrit smiles and I luv her so much.

26

Sumtime Mummy ly down and clos her eye and she luk like Mary, who I saw in a cherch in a candel lite, but I dont remembr were. But Mummy luk so luvly and cuddly it make me trembul with joy. Dont you think that Mummy is the most butefull one in all the world? Ah but I am going to tell you sum more. I told Neels how luvly Mummy is and Neels told Mister Henriks and I here Neels say if Mummy butey corsed combustion then the hole world wuld go into flams. Neels say it is a complemant. But Neels dont now sumtims. Mummy make me berst in flams. And I ask Neels what is the most big numbre I could say for luving Mummy becase I am not very gud with sums and Neels say if I rite down "infinity" that is the most big. But it dont luk very big but milions and milions of them wold be, but I luv Mummy so much and I will rite sum more.

Mummy is not like no one els becas she dont have to speak if she dont want to. And somtime it is nice when she dont speak and somtime it is nice when she do speak. Becas when she dont speak, Mummy smile and this is very good. Mummy has got a speshul smile and you dont no where it is going to start. Somtime it start from her toes and somtime from her finger and

27

somtime from her tummy and then it pop out of her eye and out of her mouth and this is very nice becas you now it is coming and you wate for it to cume. So it cum like a pressant wich is a big sirprise. And wat is nice about Mummy is watever she do is like a pressant. And wen you think about Mummy this is good too. When you think about peple you can think bad thing and narsty thing like hurt and pane and sick, but when you think about Mummy, you cant. And you can only think nice thing that are happy like Mister God. And warm. And how nice to be me, becas if I was not me I would not know, would I?

Oh dear, ther is so many things I wish I culd say, but I do not know how to say becas how can you say about love with a pensel and a paper becas you can not reely. But you can try, cant not you, so I will try.

Love is a very funy thing becas you cant see it and you cant here it and you cant tuch it when it belongs to you. So how do you know you have got it? Well I will tell you. When Neels say to me pretend you have for sweets in one hand and six sweets in another hand, how many have you got? So I say I have not got none, becas I have not and if I say I have got some, it is a lie and this is bad to do. Wen someone say I love you Anna, how do I know if it is true?

3

The Very Very First

The Bible at home was one of those huge brass-bound books. It was from this that Anna read or was read to. Seated at the table she worked her way through some of the passages of the Bible. At School and at Church she was told which passages to read; at home she was free to read whatever she wanted to. This meant that she was often puzzled as to the meaning and I had to do my best to help her understand. Trying to understand that Adam knew Eve was not the same as Anna knew Fynn, or that God asked Adam, "Who told thee that thou wast naked?" and caused her many problems.

The more she read the more puzzled she became. Often she was presented with passages that simply did not make sense to her, passages that seemed to contradict other passages. Like Luke 2:23 – "Every male that openeth the womb shall be called holy to the Lord." And Luke 23:29 – "Blessed are the barren and the wombs that never bare."

It seemed to Anna that the Bible was sometimes a bit muddled and that it asked more questions than it answered, but whatever its shortcomings, it was beautiful and since for her beauty was all important, there was no reason why she should not add her own idea of beauty to it.

Perhaps the most exciting thing about Anna was how she always managed to put together to her own satisfaction various ideas that in the normal course of education would have been frowned on. On one occasion she glued together shadows, mathematics, God and sundry ideas, to my delight and her satisfaction. It happened like this –

One evening I had been explaining to Anna how to tell the time from a sundial. Early next morning I took her to see the sundial in the local churchyard. I pointed to the part that cast the shadow and said this is called the "Gnomon". As usual, I had to write this word down on a piece of paper. Later that day the word Gnomon had to be looked up in the dictionary. The definition read "That part of a parallelogram left over when a similar parallelogram is taken from its corner".

This idea was passed over for about a year until it became another idea to work on. What excited her was the fact that it came from a Greek word meaning "Indicator".

As she carefully wrote this down on her piece of paper, her eye caught the next word "Gnosis" – knowledge of spiritual mysteries.

This bit of information made Anna search for all the words that started with the letters GN, which you must admit is an odd combination. All these words were carefully written down – gnarled, gnash, gnat, gnathic, gnaw, gneiss, gnome, gnomic, gnomon, gnosis, gnu.

Anna felt that these strange words which all started with GN ought, because of their very strange beginnings, to have something in common. And then – on the same page, was the word GOD. I did try to explain to her, but it was no use, she had found her clue, the GN words now made sense.

Serendipity is the faculty of making happy and unexpected discoveries by chance.

On one evening we were scribbling numbers and ideas on pieces of paper. I was trying to explain to Anna the mysteries of the binary system by asking the question what is the fewest number of weights and what is the value of the weights that would enable you to weigh anything up to 1,000 lbs in steps of 1 lb; after a little while she grasped the idea of how to "do it":

1, 2, 4, 8, 16, 32, 64, 128, 256, 512.

It was then quite clear to her that these 10 weights could weigh up to 1,023 lbs. This was certainly one of those beautiful things that had to be written down and treasured.

All this was nice and organized, but things are not always quite like you work them out. The greengrocer in the market didn't do things quite like that. Anna took me to the market place to show me this new miracle. On our workings out we had put the article to be weighed in the left hand pan and the weights in the right hand pan, but the man in the market place wasn't doing this, for he seemed to put weights in either pan. It certainly looked as if the man was cheating, so we went back to working it out again. In the first case we only put the weights in the right hand pan, and in the second case you could put the weights in the right hand pan or maybe the left hand or sometimes even both, and the numbers we had found for the first case certainly didn't work in the second case, so I had to explain how to work out these other weights, and they turned out to be 1, 3, 9, 27, 81, 243, 729.

This is a story about the very very first. Mister God is very very old, but a long time ago he was yung and before that he was only a baby and before that he was not even born and their was not a world and their was not a star and there was not anything.

But there was Mister God's Mummy and Daddy. But you could not see them. And you could not see them because they was so big.

If you have a very little thing, you have to go very clos before you can see it and if you go far away, you cant. If you have a montain wich is big you cant see the top if you are clos, but you can if you go far away and this is like Mister God's Mummy and Daddy. You cant go far away from them, so you cant see them. If you go too far away, you can see them but you get very lonly, so you cant. So you have to stay very clos and you know they are there but you cant see them, so that is why they had a little baby.

Well, you see, when the little baby GOD was getting redy to be born he was in his mummy woom, that is were all the babys is made. It is very dark in there. When the baby GOD was born, then he must have some light and when his Mummy and Daddy had a party to selebrate with all the angles, they put lots and lots of light in the sky and make it look pritty and this is stars. The Mummy and Daddy are very polite and teech the little baby GOD to be polite too and to say "If you please" and "No thank you" and thing like that. The little GOD have all the thing he want. A gold spoon and a gold plate and a gold chair and everything and then he want a ball to play with, so his Mummy tuk a lot of dirt and spit on it and roll it into a ball and this is the world, so you can see how big the little baby GOD is.

All the thing was very pritty. And because the little GOD was very polite and kind he want to share all the thing, so he told his Mummy and his Mummy say I cant make you a little brother and sister because it take such a lot of time. And the little GOD said "Oh dere what shall I do"?. And the Mummy say "I have got a good idea" and she tuk off the table a looking glas and say "What can you see?". So the little GOD look and say I can see my face, it is a reflekshun. And Mummy say "Can you play with yor reflekshun?" and the little GOD say "How can I share all the pritty thing with my reflekshun? That is greedy". And it is too!

Then the Mummy say "Do you know where you come from?" and the little GOD say "Yes, I come from yor woom" and the Mummy smile a big smile and say, "Yes, but first you come from a pictur in my hart and the picktur in the hart come true if you love them enogh. What is the picktur in yor hart little one?". And the little GOD say "Ther is a picktur of people and animal and I want to share all this pritty things and you and Daddy and all the angels with the animals and people".

In the night time all the picktur come true becase the little God love them so much. And all the people and animals come out of the little God's hart. And you know your hart is not very big, so you can see for milions of people and animals to cum out, they must be very tiny and so they were. Well, at the very first everybody was happy and the little GOD teech the people to talk and play musik and make things and everybody was happy because all the people could see him.

But when the little God grow up, he got so big that nobody could see him and all the people tuk the pritty things and say "This is mine". Of corse, they wasnt but that is what they said and then they got greedy and greedy and then start to hit each other and throw stomes and make boms. Because the little GOD grow up and got so big that they culdn't see him and they neerly forgot him.

So a lot of people make a statoor of GOD small enogh to see and then another lot of people make another statoor of GOD and then they fite to see what statoor is best. And they make boms and guns and a lot of peple is hurt and it is very silly because Mister God is much bigger than statoors.

Well, Mister God luvs peple very much, so he says "I know what, people cant see me because I am too big, so I will send my little baby boy who is the rite sise". So he send his little baby boy who is called Jether to a lady called Mary to luk arfter and Mister God say "That is all rite now, Jether is just the rite sise". And you would think that was the end, would not you? Arfter all the trubble Mister God tuk, woodnt you? But it wasnt, Oh no!

Anna very rarely used the name Jesus; she preferred the name Jether, which she found in the Concordance. This is the next name in the list of proper names in the Concordance. Its meaning is "He that excels or remains; or that examines, searches: or a line or string".

It was the idea of "line or string" that so attracted Anna. We had often spent hours lying on the deck of a deep water sailing vessel, listening to Niels's explanation of what all the ropes and gear were for. The fact that every rope had a place and a purpose, and that Englishmen, Frenchmen and Germans, every nationality, understood where the rope for a certain sail was to be found, was sufficient for Anna to rename Jesus as Jether. Kurt, a German sailor, told Anna she was "wider sinn", that is to say "against the sense".

When Jether was a man, he started to tell all the peple about Mister God, but a lot of peple didnt want to here because first Mister God was too big and then he was too little and peple are eccasperating. They dont know what they want. And Jether keep on telling the people "You have got to becum little Or you wont know". And they want to be big alredy, And you cant, becase Fansy being born full sise! Then a lot of people cort Jether and put nales in him and stuck him on a tree and stuck sords in him and then he was ded. All because he wasnt big enogh. Some of the people nearly know him, but not qite and like the statoors of Mister GOD they was rong. So they had another fite and this time a worse fite called a war and this time with tank and aroplane and peple keep on fiteing because they dont know what sise they are and they are silly, becase Mister God and Jether and Vrach and all the angels are so luving. So I will tell you sum story about them.

Vrach was Anna's own spelling of the Hebrew word *Ruach*, meaning spirit or breath, which was used in the Old Testament but linked with the Holy Spirit of the New Testament. I was surprised these words – Vrach, Jether – were so important to her, but felt that she had to find her way, in her own words, in her relationship with Mister God.

If you dont know what Mister God and Jether and Vrach look like I will tell you. Now I will tell you about Mister God first. He dont luk like me and you. He has not go no arms and legs and no face and no body like me and you so you will know he luk diffrent but he luk very luvley all the sam.

If you go for a walk you see a lot of things and you think a lot of things in yore hed. Well one of the things you think of is going home. So then you think it is a long way away and all the thinks is insid you and yore home is outsid you. So when you go home, all your think cum out of you and yor home go insid you, you see. Wen I am not with Mummy I have a lot of think in my hed, I think I wish I culd hold Mummy hand and I wish I culd kiss Mummy and I wish I culd tuch Mummy, but it all stay in my hed. But when I go home, it all come out of my hed, becase I do it. And when I do, Mummy go insid me and I go insid Mummy. If I dont go insid Mummy, how can I luk at me because I luk the rong way. So when I luv Mummy then I go insid her and luk out out of her eye and see me and see how much Mummy luv me and this is very nice and thriling.

If someone luv you they let you cum insid. But if they dont luv you, they dont. Well Mister GOD is like that to. He let you com insid and see yourself, but you got to let MISTER GOD cum in too, becase he want to luk out to see himself. You see, MISTER GOD dont like no reflekshun and if he dont luk out of peples eye, how do he know what peple think of him? and this is the only way MISTER GOD can see himself. If you luk in a luking glas and see yor face reflekshun and then wink yore rite eye, the reflekshun wink the othre one, but if you see yor reflekshun wink its rite eye then you know it is not a reflekshun, but you.

4

The Story of Fin

This is a story of Fin. Some people do not know how Fin is and I am sad for that because Fin is the best person in all of the world. Fin is very big and very strong but he is very delikat and very gentle. And he can frow me rigte up in the air lik a bal and catsh me too. He is like a butefall flowre made from stone.

Fin say if you live in a howse and you let the window get sploshd and dirty and if you look out of the window it look like the world is dirty, but it is not. If you look inside it look dirty too but it is not dirty becase the window is dirty. Well I will say sum more of Fin becase Fin say all of the peple have two windows. First all peple have got eye window and then a hart window. The eye window is to look out and seen thing from and the hart window is to see inside to see you. Fin say wen you cry it is for to wash the window so you can see better.

One day I ask Fin for som sweet and Fin say no and I was sad and I cry som ters and I cry som ters to wash my eye window becas my eye window was all dirty, dirty with greedy for sweets. And Fin did not say nothing and Fin piket me up and put me to a luking glas to see my face reflecshun and it was all funy like rain on a hows window. And I culd not see proper and then I stop the cry and see Fin face reflecshun and it was all smilig. And so I smile too and then I see my eye sparklin becas I can see good. And then I see that Fin say no, becas he have got no mony, becas he give it all to Missis Barkr to buy som penuts to sell to get som mony to buy som food and I did not see good, becase I have got a dirty eye window and it was all splosht with greedy dirty.

43

Mrs Barker was a little old lady who sold peanuts outside the cinemas called the Coliseum and the Palladium in the Mile End Road. One day I found her without any stock – so we took a tram towards Aldgate and bought about £3 worth of peanuts, which we brought back to her.

Everbody has got a eye window and a hart window. Fin teech me how to clean my eye window and my hart window. And if you know Fin then you have got a very speshal Fin window. And this is very nice to have. If you take some dirt to Fin he say about it and make it lik dimons and if you take to Fin a tram tiket he make it like a butefall piktur. Fin is very very speshal and very very butefall but you have to be little inside or you can not see propre.

Anna and I explored dirt under the miscroscope, where anything seemed to be transformed. The tram tickets were of different colours and collected from the streets very easily, so they could be used to make patterns, or folded into complicated paper chains and even turned into Christmas decorations.

One day Fin was very sad becase Danny was kild with a big stiker [knife]. So in the nighte I crep in bed with Fin. Fin go to slep and I then see the ters on his face becase we have a stret lighte in the stret to see with. I cry a bit too becase I was sad for Danny.

There is on thing abot Fin. A lot of time he is not full up with his self but is full up of som othre people. Som time he is just full up of his self. I like this time best of all becase I do not want to see no thing els and I am full up of laghin. I ask Fin can I have a nothre name and Fin say yes I can have two names. One is Mowse, becase Fin say I crep in his hart and make a nest ther. And the nothre name is Joy becase I make him hapy and I am very glad for that becase that is very very holy.

Somtime I think that Fin is an angel. If you want to know the diffrence from a person and an angel I will tell you. An angel is easy to get inside of, and a person is not. Every bit of an angel is inside and every bit of a person is not and most of a person is outside.

45

One person who is very specal is dere Fin. It is like loking at the very very inside of love. All the thing are nice to do with Fin and some of the thing are very nice an specal.

One of the nice things is to go for a walk with Fin in the simitery [cemetery]. Only Fin do not call it a simitery. Fin call it an orchard, becase Mister God come to pick up the sols when they are redy like aples. I like going to the orchard with Fin becase there is no one ther, only ded one and Mister God and sols. Fin say no on go to the orchard becase people are afrade to be ded, but I am not afrade becase the orchard is very butefall and ther is millon of flowre and it is sily to be a frade to be ded in all them flowre. When we go to the orchard Fin tell the name and how old and wen they was ded and ther are a lot of little children ded in the orchard. Only they are not ther no more, but they are in heven. When Fin tells the name, I say hello Susan this is Anna and Fin talking and then I say how butefall the orchard is and thing like that and then we say a litle prer and say will you give all our lov to Mister God and to Jether and to Vrach and to all the angel and to all the peple. What I am sory for is Judas and Pontas Pirot and all the peple that put

Jether on the cross. And one day I cry in the orchard for them and Fin cudle me and then say we rite all the names of them on som paper and put it in a tin and put in the holy ground and leeve it to Mister God. Fin say every peple have got a bit of Judas inside and a bit of Pontos pilot inside and every peple put a nother nale in Jether.

Fin say one thing to remmber and this is it. If it is good to do, then do it, if it is not good to do, then do not do it. And so I say how do I know if it is good and Fin say it is easy. Do not git stuck inside of you, com out and go inside of peple and animles and flowres an trees and see if you like it and if you do like it, then it is good and if you do not like it, then it is bad. If you pertend to be a cat and you kik it, it hert, so it is bad. If you stroke it, it is nice, so it is good. Fin say if you lok at a howse on the outside it is a howse, but if you look at a howse on the inside, it is not a howse but it is a home. And that is like peple. If you lok at one on the outside it is a person, but if you lok at one in the inside then it has got a reel name. And so has everything got a reel name. Even flee and spidre. And Fin say somtime this is hard to lern, to see inside a thing. Somtime you can not tell becase a church look like a mewseum and lik a flic hows and you can not tell from the outside, but you can only tell from the inside and that is wat to be alive is.

Oh Oh Oh I do love Fin very much and I ask Mister God evernighte if I can marry Fin and have a hows and som baby too. If I am six and Fin is tweny then I can mary Fin when I am tweny and Fin is tirthy fore. I ask Jacky and Sally and Corry if they marry Fin first can I too and they say yes.

For nerly everbody down our stret say up the top [of the street] is bad, but it is not becase Fin say it is not bad. Nerly everbody say they are very wicked and they are not wicked becase Fin say we must not say that. Only Mister God can say that and Mister God is very good.

At the top corner of the street was a house that was a lot bigger than the rest. In this house lived Milly, Sally, Corey, and a few other young ladies. The fact that these young ladies were for the most part prostitutes was the reason why it was commonly called the "dirty house". Anna had a vague idea of what it meant but that was no reason why she couldn't be friends with the girls. In fact, she thought that Milly, who was usually known as the Venus de Mile

End, was the most beautiful girl in the world and I would never have argued with that. The care and protection that these girls gave to Anna could not have been sweeter. I had known them for a number of years, and I knew them as very good friends. Given other circumstances they would have been different, but with poor homes, little education, and even less money, prostitution was the only way they knew how to make money. I have known these young ladies save over £200 to send little Maria to have her leg corrected after the ravages of rickets. It was more than I could have done.

Many times Anna and I have sat with them and so often the talk turned to the subject of religion and God. The passing years have made me realize that they were among the few people who could admit to themselves that they were sinners, but then they had families to keep and it was the only way they knew how.

Anna's friendship with these young prostitutes taught her a lot – perhaps a bit too much, who knows. I do know that they were always very careful in what they said when Anna was around, but things slip out occasionally and Anna, like most children, would often repeat what she had heard the older people say without knowing what was meant by it.

What was puzzling for me was the fact that some of the girls's customers did regard themselves as good solid citizens, to say nothing of good churchgoers, but that was my problem, not Anna's. For her the girls were just nice to be with. What puzzled Anna was how such nice people could be called "dirty". Anna would have none of it, neither would I. Milly taught Anna how to make bead belts, necklaces and bracelets. All the adults for streets around knew what the girls did, but it was only Anna and her friends and me who knew what they could do. They were a bit special to those of us who knew them and definitely not dirty.

One of the thing that make me very sad is this. I wuld like all the big girls up the top to have real propre sweet love. Fin culd do it so gentle and sweet and culd make the big girls so hapy and holy and it wuld be so lovly.

Fin go up the top to see them and Fin mummy say I can go too and Fin mummy rote this on some paper and say to put it in my book. If they are blind, give them your hand, if they are only in the dark, give them a candel. And then she laft out loud and say a candel calld Anna.

5

Once Upon A Time

Whenever Anna was confronted by the latest miracle or had one of those very important children's questions to ask, she wrote it into a little story. This could be very confusing, since you could not ask a question of an oak tree that was meant for a beech tree, neither could you ask a black cat exactly the same question you could ask a ginger cat. Her little stories were nearly always about some aspect of a thing or person.

This habit of writing about some aspect of a thing or a person meant that there could be as many as ten or more little stories about dogs or whatever, which had to be put together before any one could understand her more complete picture of dogs, or whatever she was writing about.

Anna's "Once upon a Time" was the result of many, many little stories that were finally put together after a long time. This putting together was a very solitary and intense activity which could totally absorb her for many days. Nothing was allowed to intrude into this part of Anna's life. It took me some while to realize how important this "putting together time" was for her.

Since those days I have heard Anna's "putting together time" called by many names, but I still think "Talking with God" is the best I've found so far!

When I wok up in the morning it was stil neerly dark and it was just becuming ligte and I thort this is not a nice day. So I pull the sheets over my hed and just my nos wos out and then I here sumthing. It was going drip, drip, drip. And then I was very sad becase I thort it sownd like all the angels criing. But then I here it more drip, drip, drip, so then I no it was rain that was making the noise.

When I luk out of the widow I see the sun was all like blood and all the miss was everwere and it was very cold to get out of bed and as I stud at the window I fel my tows get cold and I think of my bed wich is warm so I go bake

54

to bed were it is nise and warm. Then I put my nos under the shets and I lissen to the bird sing in the tree and wunder why bird sing wen the day is so bad.

So then I thort I would like Mummy to make me warm and I thort I wold like to kis Mummy, but it was so cold I did not want to go out of my bed. And I thort soon Mummy will cum out of bed and cum to kiss me, so I wate and think of Mummy to cum to put her arms rownd me and to kiss me and I think how nice it is. So all my tows kirl and so do I like a bal and so I wate.

Then I here a funy thing and it go swiss, swiss, swiss. It is like the wind but it is not the wind. Then a sonbem cum in the windo and hit me in the face, so I jump out of bed and see a sunbem rite up from the clowds and on the sunbem was a man. The man was showting Were is lazy Anna? were is lazy Anna? and all the bird and all the rabit and all the bear say it too and I wonder becase I am Anna, but I am not lazy and then the man slid down the sonbem rite in my room and say, There is lazy Anna! Then I see the man is

Mister Vrach, so I say I am not lazy and you must not say that becase we are frends. You are lazy say Vrach. You must com with me. And then I say, I wate for Mummy so I cant come. Yes you will com and Vrach pickt me up and went all up the sunbem again. Wen we got to the top of the sunbem Vrach say, This is a lazy werld for lazy children and you are lazy and wen you are not lazy I will take you home again. And then he went away.

It was very cold and I was very lonly, so I sit down becas I was sad. And then I here a lot of peple talking but it was not peple, so I luk, but it was not there, and then I know the talking is in the grownd and in the air. So I put my eer on the grownd and lissen and I here it say It is very cold today so I wont grow today. So then I say Who is talking in the grownd? And it say Who is that? and I say It is Anna. Who is talking in the grownd? And it say I am a little flowre seed. Why dont you want to grow today? Becase it is too cold and I am warm in my bed, so I will grow two times as much the nex day. But it will be cold the next day too. Then I will stay in bed again, say the little seed. But if all the seeds stay in bed there will not be any spring and a little seed cant grow two times as much in one day. But he did say noting becase he gon to sleep agan and I thort the seeds are sily and lazy.

Then I went to walk but all the things was stil and lazy. The tree wuld not grow and the leeves would not open and the bird would not sing and it was a very sad werld.

Them I cum to a river that was not going, so I say River why are you not going? and the river say Becase I am lazy. And soon I cum to a waterfal, but the water do not fall, but stay in the air and I say Waterfal, why do you not fall? and the waterfal say Becase I am lazy. But you must fall, say Anna, becase a waterfal must larf and play and go gugle gugle gugle and if you dont then how can you be a waterfal? O, says the waterfal, I did not think of that and he start to cry and sum little drips of water fall down and mak a little pule and so I cry, O plese mister waterfal, dont cry becase waterfal is hapy thing, not sad thing. So then he stop and say, O Anna if you culd mak me larf then I wuld be a reel waterfal agan. So I thort very hard and said Mister Waterful I will tell you a funy story. Say wen you are redy. And the Waterfal say I am redy. So I begin.

Once upon a time and the Waterful go Gug gug gug gugel gugel gugel and start to fall down and start to larf so much I am splosht with all the water and the waterful say Ha! Ha! Ha! Ho! Ho! Ho! Anna! that is a very funy story! But I do not know what it is to larf at becase I have not start the story yet. So I say I have not start the story yet. But the waterful larf mor and more. Then a little bear com out of a hole and say Mister Waterful Wat do you larf about? and the waterful say Ho! Ho! Ho! little bear Anna has told me a very funny story. And the little bare say Wat is the funy story? tell it to me, so I can larf too. So the Waterful say, Anna say Once upon a time. Then the little bare larf and larf and larf til he fall over and roll on the grownd and say Ho! Ho! Ho! Anna say Once upon a time! Then a little bird start to larf and then a little rabit start to larf and the little flowr seeds com out of the grownd to see why all things was larfin for. And then all the trees and flowrs larf and larf and say, Anna say Once upon a time! and all the forest tingl with larfin, but I do not know why.

So I sit on the gras. I am a maze. Then a lot of angels cum dansing and singing in the Forest and all the forest was a-wak and was not lazy any mor,

so I get up and say to the angel Eccuse me, if you plese, why is all thing larfin? So the angel say Becase you tell a funy story. But I did not start it even. I only say Once upon a time. Then the angles say That is what is funy, you see, Anna. You can not be twise upon a time. Then the angle dans away, but I stil do not think it is funy. So I sit down agan and I think and think and think and then I know. Of cors you can not be twise upon a time becos you can not do two thing at a time.

So I get up and ran and call Mister Vrach I am not lazy no mor. And then ther was a swiss, swiss, swiss and Mister Vrach say Ho! Ho! Ho! Anna you are not lazy no more. Wat did you lern? and so I say I lern I was lazy becase I wantd to kiss Mummy but I was too lazy to get from my bed becase it was cold but wate for Mummy to come to me. Then Mister Vrach say Becase you have lern very good I will give you a pressant Anna. Wot wuld you like? So I say Mister Vrach will you take me back to the very beginning? So Mister Vrach take me to the top of the sonbem and smile a very big smile and kiss me and then puss me very hard down the sonbem and I was going fast and fast and fast and I was most brethles and then ther was a bump and I was in my bed agan.

Then I open my eye and it was just becuming ligte and I hear drip, drip, drip and then a sonbem com in the winder so I ran to the winder and see a man on the sonbem and he wave to me and all the little bird sing and then my tows get very cold, becas it is very cold, but I am very warm inside and I want to kiss Mummy very much and I do not care how cold it is. So I ran to Mummy room and jump to bed with Mummy and kiss her very much becase I am full up of love and Mummy hug me very tite and I am very happy and then Mummy say, Anna it will be a very nice day and I say Yes Mummy! and larf becase it neerly was not.

The end

6

The Tree

I saw a lovly tree today
So lovly that it made me pray
The lefs was all harts and lovly gren
The most lovly tree that you have ever seen
It mad my hart sing and my hed go hummy
So I tuk some off to gift to Mummy
And wen I did it make her smile
And I think that is very werth while
And do you know that Mister God
Made a big smile and gift his hed a nod